C000261469

MU

Tom Wainwright

MUSCLE

A one-act comedy

OBERON BOOKS
LONDON

WWW.OBERONBOOKS.COM

First published in 2011 by Oberon Books Ltd
521 Caledonian Road, London N7 9RH
Tel: +44 (0) 20 7607 3637 / Fax: +44 (0) 20 7607 3629
e-mail: info@oberonbooks.com
www.oberonbooks.com

Copyright © Tom Wainwright 2011

Tom Wainwright is hereby identified as author of this play in accordance with section 77 of the Copyright, Designs and Patents Act 1988. The author has asserted his moral rights.

All rights whatsoever in this play are strictly reserved and application for performance etc. should be made before commencement of rehearsal to United Agents, 12-26 Lexington Street, London, W1F 0LE. No performance may be given unless a licence has been obtained, and no alterations may be made in the title or the text of the play without the author's prior written consent.

This book is sold subject to the condition that it shall not by way of trade or otherwise be circulated without the publisher's consent in any form of binding or cover or circulated electronically other than that in which it is published and without a similar condition including this condition being imposed on any subsequent purchaser.

A catalogue record for this book is available from the British Library.

ISBN: 978-1-84943-093-7

Cover image by Cherie Wren.

Printed in Great Britain by CPI Antony Rowe, Chippenham.

Characters

STEVE (early-thirties)

TERRY (early-thirties)

DAN (early-thirties)

Muscle was first produced at the Bristol Old Vic Studio on the 8th September 2009. The cast was

STEVE:	Sion Pritchard
TERRY:	Paul Mundell
DAN:	Stewart Wright

Director, Lee Lyford
Designer, Hayley Grindle

The production was remounted by Hull Truck Theatre in February 2011 with the same cast, director and designer.

A gym. Sparse stage. A few benches. Upstage area is the changing room. All the use of equipment is mimed.

(STEVE enters changing room. Looks lost, checking the place out. Catches sight of himself in the mirror. Falters. Looks at belly. Hears TERRY from off, checks himself then addresses TERRY who is entering.)

STEVE: Come on then, dickhead, get your tits out. *(TERRY looks at him.)* What? You know you want to. Dragging me down here on a Saturday afternoon for a bit of you and me time, eh? Bit of "quality" time eh? Go on, show us your arse. *(Shouts.)* I WANT TO SEE YOUR BOTTOM.

TERRY: Good one, Steve. Real cool.

STEVE: D'you think so?

TERRY: Yeah. Smooth.

STEVE: I thought so too. Here, Terry. Do you want to see my belly button?

TERRY: Shut up, Stephen.

STEVE: Oooo. *(Pause. Circles TERRY.)*. Imitating T's accent. "I don't shut up, I grow up, and when I look at you, I throw up."

TERRY: Brilliant.

STEVE: "*Brilliant.* My name's Terry, and I think everything's *brilliant.*" Ooh look…he's taking his shirt off. Get ready, it's coming…and it's off! And the pigeon chest is out. Still no hairs on his chest, but he can't help that – he's only nine.

TERRY: *(Claps him.)*

STEVE: Random applause from Terry. Good to see he can still have a sense of humour in spite of it all. Ooh and here come the trousers. *(They get a bit stuck.)* Don't tease us Terry, we want to see your buns –

TERRY: What if somebody comes in?

STEVE: Oh shit. Are you scared?

7

TERRY: What?

STEVE: It's scary isn't it?

TERRY: It would just be embarrassing if someone comes in
with me in me half-naked and you screaming like a small
child.

STEVE: Then put some clothes on you dirty little boy.

TERRY: Are you going to get changed?

STEVE: Would you like that? Would you like to see me slip
into something a little more "comfortable"? You would
wouldn't you, you little tiger.

TERRY: Do you not think you might be a bit hot like that?

STEVE: You got me hot, baby.

TERRY: Steve.

STEVE: I'm changed, man, I'm changed. I've got layers. Got to
work up a bit of a sweat before I get my bod out. Besides,
you might try and bum me, I know what you're like.

*(TERRY is now fully naked. He was not wearing any underpants.
STEVE goes quiet until TERRY has put some more clothes on. When
he has, STEVE jumps up onto a bench and blows his hair
back with a hairdryer.)*

STEVE: *(American accent.)* Terry, Terry, it's me, Steve! Terry,
I just want you to know, all those things I said, I didn't
mean them. I didn't mean any of it. I was angry. People say
hurtful things when they're angry and I'm sorry, Terry. I'm
sorry I hurt you. But I can't believe this is supposed to be
the end of us. Surely we're stronger than that? We can start
over, I know we can. Please come back, I can't live without
you, you're my sun, my moon, I LOVE YOU TERRY! –

TERRY: *(Snatches and turns off hairdryer.)* Stop it! You're making
a complete embarrassment out of yourself. What if
somebody walks in?

STEVE: I thought we'd been through this, Terry.

TERRY: Seriously, man, you're behaving like a kid. You're here as my guest. I don't want to get barred from this place because you couldn't stop dicking around.

STEVE: You know you're quite sexy when your angry.

TERRY: I give up.

STEVE: Oh don't give up Terence, you've got your whole life ahead of you. I'm sorry you find it so distressing that I have to come here as your "guest". It must be a terrible burden for you. *(Pause.)* Do you want me to go outside and pay?

TERRY: Of course I don't but… look if you're here on my ticket I'm responsible for you, you know? If you start screaming and shouting it's me they pick up for it, not you.

STEVE: I hadn't thought about that. That's quite serious.

TERRY: Steve –

STEVE: No really, man, if you get "picked up" for that you could go down for a long time.

TERRY: I'm going.

STEVE: Alright, man, don't worry, I'll stop farting about. I'll try not to get you thrown out of here, OK? I'll try my extra best. *(Massages his shoulders.)*. You need to take it easy, mate, you'll give yourself an aneurysm. Come on, now: who's your Daddy?

TERRY: I'm your Daddy.

STEVE: Hello, Daddy.

TERRY: Come here, boy.

(They laugh.)

STEVE: Come on, tiger, lets go and lift some *weights*.

(TERRY walks into gym.)

I'm just going to get changed. I'll catch you up.

(STEVE removes tracksuit to reveal a ridiculous outfit and enters gym; meanders about, a bit unsure. TERRY stretches, doing Salute to the Sun progressions.)

What you doing? Oi...what you doing?

TERRY: *(Straining.)* Stretching.

STEVE: *(Mimics.)* Oh. Are you stretching?

(STEVE watches TERRY for a while.)

"And in...and out...and in...and out...don't forget to breathe.

Diaphragm down. Keep the shoulders aligned."

(Suddenly, when TERRY is on the ground....)

Come on Terry, You can do it! GO! GO! GO! Work it, baby. I know everybody says you're a whoopsie, but you're going to show them aren't you? Nobody *stretches* like Terry Furnace. Look at the arch in that man's back – have you seen his breath control? Gay? Gay? What's gay about going to a gym and not lifting any weights? Who needs weights when you can *stretch?!*

TERRY: *(Quiet.)* Steve, you're doing my head in. Please stop. *(STEVE looks at him.)* Really, I'm just going to leave if you carry on.

(Pause.)

STEVE: OK, man. OK.

(Silence.)

TERRY: I'm sorry –

STEVE: No, it's cool.

(Silence.)

TERRY: What you going to do?

STEVE: Eh?

TERRY: *(Looking around.)* What are going to work on?

STEVE: Oh…er *(Looks around.)* Don't know. I've got a bit of a bad back actually.

TERRY: Really?

STEVE: Yeah…just…pulled it the other day doing some… stuff. Still a bit niggly actually. Think I'll do some leg work actually…Yeah, do a bit of leg-work I reckon. Work on my quads and my thighs a bit.

TERRY: OK.

(STEVE shapes up to do what might be some squats.)

Make sure you keep your back straight.

STEVE: Eh?

TERRY: When you're squatting. Are you doing some squats?

STEVE: Yeah.

TERRY: Cool.

(STEVE does some squats half-heartedly. Then stops.)

STEVE: Do you want some water? I'm getting some water, do you want some?

TERRY: I'll grab some in a bit.

STEVE: Are you sure?

TERRY: Yeah.

(STEVE goes to get some water. TERRY moves over to the bench press.)

STEVE: What you doing?

TERRY: Gonna work on my upper body.

STEVE: On the press bench?

TERRY: The bench press, yeah.

STEVE: Right…Do you want a hand?

TERRY: Eh?

STEVE: Do you want me to spot you?

TERRY: No it's fine, Steve.

STEVE: No come on, man, it's dangerous pressing on your own.

TERRY: I'm not going to be lifting anything heavy…

STEVE: Even still I know what you're like, margarine boy. Your wrists'll snap halfway up and you'll drop the bloody bar on your face. I'll have to take you to hospital, the whole thing'll be an ugly mess…

TERRY: Do you *want* to help me?

STEVE: Only if you want me to.

TERRY: Well, I don't mind.

STEVE: It's up to you.

TERRY: I'm probably alright.

STEVE: Oh. OK.

TERRY: I didn't mean…you can help me if you like…

STEVE: Well, no, it was only if you wanted a hand, but…you're obviously OK, so…

TERRY: No, give me a hand, that'd be great. Cheers.

STEVE: Yeah?

TERRY: Yeah.

STEVE: OK then, up you get soldier. *(Moves behind bench.)* Let's see what you're made of? How does this work – what's this? *(TERRY lifts bar off.)* Right you are. OK then – lovely. You don't mind if I talk to you as you go, offer you a bit of encouragement? You probably need all the help you can get, my little flower.

TERRY: Steve.

STEVE: I'm sorry. I'm sorry. In your own time, mate.

(STEVE "spots" TERRY at the bench press.)

I don't say a word. I walk straight up to him and then bam *(Mimes head butt.)* right on the nose bridge. Feel that slender bit of cartilage splinter under my forehead and his warm blood shower down my face.

Now he's ready, now he's scared. His eyes are trying to make friends with me, pleading like a puppy, confused and upset. He doesn't want any trouble, he didn't know anything about me – bam, bam, bam, shut the fuck up you runt. He's on his knees now, he's crying. I stick my chin in his face and say, "Hit me. Fucking hit me," but he's too much of a pussy to even do that. I'm going to kick him in the face. I'm going to smash my foot into his big horrible face. Bam. The blood splatters thick against the bar as he flips backwards. Out cold now, and I'm standing over him screaming, "CUNT, CUNT, CUNT!"

(They collapse in a heap. DAN enters the changing room in biking gear and gets changed. Then leaves. STEVE and TERRY recover themselves.)

STEVE: How you doing?

TERRY: Yeah. You?

STEVE: Yeah, I'm good man.

TERRY: Jesus, my leg's shaking.

STEVE: Yeah, that was pretty intense man.

(They giggle, smile. Silence.)

TERRY: Oh. *Fuck it...* Can you just...massage my shoulder – I think I've pulled something.

STEVE: Oh yeah?

TERRY: Yes, Steve, think you can manage that?

STEVE: Well, I don't know. One thing could lead to another and you know…

TERRY: OK, don't worry about it.

STEVE: I'm only joking, man, come on where does it hurt?

TERRY: No really, it's fine, I don't want you to.

STEVE: Don't be a tease…

TERRY: Don't fucking touch me!

STEVE: OK.

(*Pause.*)

Where is it…? Is it… (*Gestures behind his shoulder.*)

TERRY: …yeah…

STEVE: …yeah…that's a sod that….Do you want me to…?

TERRY: Yeah. If you don't mind.

STEVE: No.

(*STEVE massages TERRY's shoulder.*)

TERRY: Oo…yeah…Ah.

STEVE: Yeah?

TERRY: Yeah. Yeah, that's really good.

STEVE: (*Resumes.*) Fuck I'm good to you, Terry.

TERRY: Oo yeah.

STEVE: (*Sits on bench, behind him.*) Now I don't want you getting any ideas…about you and me…you are looking rather lovely today though, Terence.

TERRY: It's alright, I think I can resist you.

(*Pause. More groans.*)

STEVE: You're just a big baby aren't you?

TERRY: Goo goo gaga goo.

(Stops massaging, stands.)

STEVE: That's a bit weird, mate. I mean *(Imitates.)*, "what if somebody walked in?"

TERRY: Fuck off.

STEVE: "Seriously, man. I don't want to get barred from this place because you couldn't stop dicking around."

TERRY: Alright, you've made your point – I feel like a cock. Are you happy?

STEVE: Extremely.

TERRY: Good.

(Pause. Massage.)

STEVE: Goo gaga goo goo *(Finds this hilarious.)*

TERRY: Stephen – I'm – incredibly – embarrassed – please – stop.

STEVE: OK, Daddy.

TERRY: Can we just let that one slide?

STEVE: Oh OK then…baby boy.

(Resumes massage.)

TERRY: Do you ever think about having kids?

STEVE: You what?

TERRY: Kids. Ever thought about them. You and Cherie.

STEVE: Bloody hell, man….

(Pause.)

Well, yeah, I've thought about it.

(Pause. Begins to massage the whole of TERRY's back, neck and head.)

STEVE: Yeah… *kids.* Might be alright. Not for a while though, eh? I've got too much punch in my pouch to settle down and have nippers, d'you know what I mean?

TERRY: Not really.

STEVE: Yes, you do.

TERRY: No, I don't.

STEVE: You know what I mean.

TERRY: Steve, I honestly don't know what you're talking about.

STEVE: Don't play the cunt with me –

TERRY: I think you'd make a great Dad.

(Pause. Massage.)

STEVE: Yeah?

TERRY: Yeah.

(Pause. Massage.)

Granted you act like an arsehole most of the time but that'd probably work in your favour. I think you'd be great.

STEVE: Fuck off. Always thought I'd be a crap Dad.

TERRY: *No.*

STEVE: It's a bollocks. I'd fuck it up.

TERRY: What do you mean you'd fuck it up?

STEVE: I'd fuck it up. *(Like a train.)* Fuck-it-up, fuck-it-up, fuck-it-up.

TERRY: No you wouldn't.

STEVE: Terry, I fuck things up: that's what I do. Ask Cherie, she'll tell you. Ask my Dad. Steve "fuck-it-up" Watson at your service. Need somebody to fuck things up for you? Steve's yer man. Just don't ask him to baby sit for your kids.

TERRY: You could baby sit my kids.

STEVE: You haven't got any kids.

TERRY: But if I did...

STEVE: But you don't and you won't and neither will I because nobody in their right mind is going to want to settle down with a pair of titheads who work out together on a Saturday afternoon.

TERRY: Thanks, mate.

STEVE: It's alright, mate.

TERRY: What about Cherie?

STEVE: What about her?

TERRY: You've settled down with her...you got married...she's your wife.

STEVE: Yes.

TERRY: Well there you go. You've got somebody.

STEVE: Yes. I have.

TERRY: She wanted to settle down with you didn't she? Didn't she?

STEVE: Yes.

TERRY: How is she, by the way?

STEVE: She's fine...

TERRY: Have you talked about kids?

STEVE: What is this obsession with kids?

TERRY: Sorry, mate, I didn't realise it was such a touchy subject.

STEVE: It's not touchy.

TERRY: Sounds pretty touchy. You're being touchy.

STEVE: I'm not touchy.

TERRY: See. Touchy. Down a bit.

(Pause.)

STEVE: Do you think I've put on weight?

TERRY: Course you have you fat bastard.

STEVE: Thanks, mate.

TERRY: It's alright, mate.

STEVE: I asked Cherie if she thought I'd put on weight.

TERRY: What did she say?

STEVE: She said she thought my body was "cute."

(Into girlfriend story. TERRY as Cherie is watching television/reading a book, lain over STEVE's lap.)

STEVE: Babe?

TERRY: Yeah?

STEVE: Have I put on weight?

TERRY: No, honey. Come here let me give you a blow job.

(TERRY gets down on his knees and starts fellating STEVE. TERRY breaks out of scenario.)

TERRY: OK, Steve, that's not what happened is it?

STEVE: No.

TERRY: No, I didn't think so.

(They start again.)

STEVE: Have I put on weight?

TERRY: No, baby. You're beautiful.

STEVE: Really?

TERRY: Yes, baby.

STEVE: I'm not as buff as I was though am I?

TERRY: Are you kidding? *(Starts to straddle STEVE.)* I want to screw you all the time. My sister wants to have a threesome with you. Would you mind? It would mean the world to her.

(Again TERRY breaks out of the scenario.)

TERRY: Steve.

STEVE: What?

TERRY: What is this?

STEVE: Sorry.

TERRY: I don't know why I bother sometimes.

STEVE: Alright, calm down. It was on the cards though.

TERRY: Bollocks.

STEVE: Please. Please.

TERRY: Last chance…I mean it.

STEVE: OK.

(They resume. This time for real. Cherie is suffering a particularly bad patch of Irritable Bowel Syndrome, which requires her to fart through most of the scene. She is watching television, lain down over STEVE's lap, who is stroking her back.)

TERRY: I'm sorry, I've got to fart.

STEVE: It's OK sweetheart, you go ahead.

TERRY: Keep rubbing.

(She farts, silently.)

STEVE: Are you…?

TERRY: *Yeah, I'm doing it.*

STEVE: Erm… Love?

TERRY: *Yeah.*

STEVE: Have I put on weight?

TERRY: Keep rubbing…what is it?

STEVE: Erm…Do you reckon I've put on a couple of pounds?

TERRY: Sure, if you want to.

(Pause.)

STEVE: Are you listening to me?

TERRY: …*yeah.*

STEVE: Well?

TERRY: *(Looks up.)* Well what?

STEVE: Have I?

TERRY: …I don't know…

STEVE: So you weren't listening. Cheers, love.

TERRY: Keep rubbing…

STEVE: Well it's true, you weren't –

TERRY: What is it? What are you talking about?

STEVE: …Do you think I've… put on weight?

TERRY: …put on weight?

STEVE: Yeah.

TERRY: …no.

STEVE: …really?

TERRY: …yes.

(Pause.)

STEVE: I don't believe you.

TERRY: Fine, why d'you bother to ask?

STEVE: I just wanted to know what you thought.

(Pause. She farts.)

STEVE: I just feel a bit…titty.

TERRY: Steve, please don't say that.

STEVE: I do. I feel wobbly all over. Look at me, I've actually got breasts. *(He squidges them together. Back to gym.)* Go on stick your dick in that.

TERRY: That's disgusting, fuck off.

STEVE: *(Laughing.)* Sorry, I couldn't help it. Do you want me to…

TERRY: Yeah, if you wouldn't mind.

STEVE: No, not at all.

(STEVE resumes massaging TERRY's head and neck.).

TERRY: So that's why you're here.

STEVE: You what?

TERRY: Shift some lard.

STEVE: Something like that. Why are you here?

TERRY: To pick guys up.

STEVE: What?

TERRY: Pick guys up.

STEVE: What, you mean…?

TERRY: Yes, that's exactly what I mean.

STEVE: *(Moving away from TERRY.)* Fuck's sake, Terry.

TERRY: You did ask.

STEVE: Fuck's sake! Why d'you bring me along if all you –

TERRY: You said you wanted to go to the gym –

STEVE: Yes, a *gym,* not some battyboy fuckfest.

TERRY: *(Explodes with laughter.)* "*Battyboy fuckfest!*"

STEVE: Shut up, man. Shut up.

TERRY: *(Recovering himself.)* I'm sorry, that's just brilliant. Do you want to go, Steve? I don't mind.

TERRY: It's just…I've agreed to meet some batty boys and have a fuckfest here a bit later so… *(STEVE pumps some iron vigorously. TERRY watches him, smiling.)*

TERRY: See look, you're going now, aren't you? You're fucking on it man.

STEVE: *(Pumping.)* FUCK OFF!

TERRY: FUCK OFF! Exactly. FUCK IT IN, STEPHEN – FUCK IT RIGHT IN!

STEVE: *(Struggling.)* Fuck…off…

TERRY: What's that, mate? I can't quite hear you…

(TERRY starts tickling him in his arm pit. STEVE shrieks, laughing and shouting, he's about to drop the bar. Ad lib. Actually drops down to his neck but TERRY catches it.)

TERRY: It's OK, sweet cheeks I gotcha.

(Lifts bar back up, STEVE tries to tickle him back around his belly.)

STEVE: Tosser.

TERRY: *(Completely unaffected.)* What are you doing, man?

STEVE: Go on you love it –

TERRY: It's not doing anything. Stop it.

STEVE: Go on you tart.

TERRY: Steve, that's my cock.

(STEVE stops. TERRY replaces bar.)

TERRY: You know I was joking…about picking guys up…it was a joke…

STEVE: Terry, she's fucking somebody else. Cherie. She's screwing somebody.

(Pause.)

TERRY: Oh no.

STEVE: Oh yes. She doesn't know that I know. She doesn't know anything.

TERRY: You haven't told her?

STEVE: No, I haven't told her.

TERRY: How long have you known?

STEVE: …couple a weeks… a month…two and a half months.

TERRY: And you haven't said anything?

STEVE: No.

TERRY: Why not?

STEVE: It's not as simple as that is it?

TERRY: Isn't it?

STEVE: No. It's not.

TERRY: Sounds pretty simple to me. She's having an affair. With another guy. Yes?

STEVE: Yes.

TERRY: And has been for at least a couple of months…

STEVE: Yes.

TERRY: Well probably more than a couple – could have been going on for…I don't know…years –

STEVE: What's your point, Terry?

TERRY: Well what are you going to do?

STEVE: What do you mean, what am I going to do?

TERRY: You have to do something.

STEVE: Why?

TERRY: Because she's having a relationship with somebody else.

STEVE: You don't understand, man. This way, I win. She doesn't know that I know. I've got the power.

TERRY: You've got the power have you, Steve?

STEVE: I've got the power.

TERRY: Yeah, you look really powerful right now. Supreme.

STEVE: I know who it is, I've seen him. I've seen *them*. I know where they've done it, I even know where they've gone for lunch afterwards. And she hasn't got a clue. She swans around the house, light as a feather, completely free; talks to me like she doesn't really know me. She's so polite – she never used to be that polite. Forever telling me she's going to the gym. I mean, what is this, why are we all going to the gym these days?

(Pause.)

TERRY: Where did they go…for lunch?

STEVE: Jesus –

TERRY: I just wondered.

STEVE: Browns, alright? They went to fucking Browns.

TERRY: Well, he's obviously got no class. Maybe if he'd taken her to Café –

STEVE: I don't care where he fucking took her for lunch, man,
I care about the fact he's screwing her – she's screwing
him. Whatever, it makes me sick.

TERRY: You've watched them…doing it?

STEVE: No, mate.

TERRY: Right. But then…?

STEVE: But then…?

TERRY: How do you…?

STEVE: I followed her. I followed her one morning: sometimes
I do that. I like watching her when she doesn't know I'm
there. Reminds me of when we first met. The back of her
head, man, it kills me. You know, with the hair all pinned
up with a few straggly bits floating down. When she does
that thing with her nose. When she's checking the traffic
before she crosses the road, going into the chemist – she
keeps going into the chemist – and then stretches her face
when she comes out. And then moves off with this very
straight back and completely still head: it's so *serious*. I…I
like it. Sometimes I see how close I can get to her without
her realising. She's got no idea and she's just…gorgeous.
It's like the calm before the storm. It sounds crazy but it's
a turn on, it's like foreplay. I can't see anything else; she's
this dirty silhouette against the grey murk. I can smell her.
Underneath her perfume, I can smell her sweat, the heat
trapped under her blouse, and I know she's got the horn, I
just know it, I can smell it. I get right behind her, pace for
pace, till her neck is literally close enough to bite, and then
I fall back. Every time, at the crucial point, I bottle it, I
can't go through with it. What I want to do is reach out and
take her, put my hand over her mouth and drag her into
an alleyway, and just…fuck her. Violently. Horribly. And
leave her there with her pants around her ankles, not even
knowing who it was. Thinking it might have been me, but
never sure. Never quite sure.

(Pause.)

TERRY: You've been stalking your own wife?

STEVE: What – no I've not been stalking her –

TERRY: And having thoughts about raping her.

STEVE: It's a fantasy man, it's supposed to be sexy, it doesn't mean I'd actually do it.

TERRY: Yes it sounds very sexy. Very erotic.

STEVE: Jesus, I wish I hadn't said anything now.

TERRY: That makes two of us.

STEVE: Oh fuck off.

(Pause.)

TERRY: Maybe you should.

STEVE: What?

TERRY: Maybe you should play out the whole rape thing. I mean ask her if she wants to do it, first. I'm not sure about the whole not-letting-her-know-it's-you part.

STEVE: Christ's sake –

TERRY: Some couples do that kind of thing. You never know…it might spice things up a bit.

STEVE: You haven't got a clue have you? Ask my wife, who's currently screwing somebody else if she'd mind if I raped her? No wonder you haven't got a….

TERRY: A boyfriend, you mean?

STEVE: Whatever, yeah.

(Pause. STEVE resumes massaging TERRY.)

When did you last make love?

STEVE: *(Moves away from TERRY.)* Oh my God –

TERRY: Well it's important –

STEVE: I don't know, alright. It's kind of been off the agenda recently.

TERRY: Maybe you should put it back on the agenda. You're not going to win her back by watching her walk down the street, looking out for alleyways…

STEVE: I guess not…

(Pause.)

TERRY: Who is it?

STEVE: Who's who?

TERRY: The guy. You said you know who he is.

STEVE: Oh, some bloke. Rides a fucking motorbike. Cunt.

TERRY: Who is he?

STEVE: Does it matter, Terry? Some bloke, that's all.

(DAN enters gym. STEVE and TERRY stare at him. Pause.)

DAN: Alright?

STEVE/TERRY: Alright?

DAN: *OK.*

(STEVE and TERRY both watch DAN as he uses a piece of equipment.)

TERRY: And what about Cherie?

STEVE: *(Patting TERRY down roughly and moving away, investigating a piece of equipment.)* What?

TERRY: Cherie.

STEVE: Cherie. *(DAN turns his head.)*

TERRY: How is she?

STEVE: She's fine, man she's fine. Don't worry about it it's fine. I shouldn't have said anything. It's fine.

TERRY: Are you going to talk to her?

STEVE: What? Erm…no. But… I will. I will.

TERRY: When?

STEVE: I don't know, mate, the conversation's not exactly flowing at the moment. Anyway, look, I didn't come here to talk about my wife. Come on, *let's do some weights, buddy.*

TERRY: Why don't you say something to her?

STEVE: (*Hushed.*) Like what, Terry? What would you say?

TERRY: I don't know. "Why are you having sex with somebody that isn't me?"

STEVE: Please shut up, man.

TERRY: But it's not very good is it, if she's sleeping with somebody else?

STEVE: No. No, it's not.

TERRY: Then why don't you say something?…Steve.

STEVE: I'm waiting for the right moment.

TERRY: The right moment?

STEVE: Yes, Terry, the right fucking moment.

TERRY: When will that be?

STEVE: I don't know, alright? I don't know anything at the moment. All I know is that I don't want to talk about it anymore. Is that OK?

TERRY: OK.

STEVE: Fantastic.

(DAN crosses in front of them to another piece of equipment. STEVE and TERRY stare.)

DAN: Alright?

STEVE/TERRY: Alright?

DAN: *OK.*

(STEVE and TERRY limber up seperately.)

TERRY: *(Noticing STEVE at a loss.)* Do you want me to show you how some of this stuff works?

STEVE: It's alright treacle, I think I can handle myself.

(STEVE goes to stepper. To DAN.)

Alright, mate?

DAN: Eh?

STEVE: Alright?

DAN: Yeah. Yeah I'm fine. Are you alright?

STEVE: Yeah, I'm alright. How about you?

DAN: Fine.

STEVE: Cool.

(STEVE puts his hands on the foot paddles and pumps his arms. After a while DAN interjects.)

DAN: Mate…Mate

STEVE: *(Bent double.)* I'm in the middle of some reps, man.

DAN: It's a stepper.

STEVE: Mate, don't interrupt me in the middle of a set.

DAN: It's a stepper. It's for your feet.

STEVE: *(Realisation. Slowly gets up.)* What, you never heard of warming up?

DAN: Is that what you were doing…warming up?

STEVE: What does it look like to you?

DAN: I don't know. I thought you might not –

STEVE: Look, mate. I know how to use a stepper, alright?

DAN: Cool.

STEVE: I used to have one at home: a stepper. Yeah, years ago…I had a stepper. One of these in fact. A *(Reads.)* 3158xl sizemaster. Classic.

DAN: You had a 3158?

STEVE: Yes I did.

DAN: Really?

STEVE: Oh yes.

DAN: That's funny.

STEVE: Yeah.

DAN: Well yeah. They only got this one in last week. It's a new piece of kit, only just come out on the market.

STEVE: *No.* Who told you that?

DAN: The manager.

STEVE: *No.* The *3158?* Nah. Been around for…nah, I used to have a stepper, had the lot mate. Stepper, bike, press bench, free-standing…

DAN: Must have cost a fair bit.

STEVE: Depends what you call a fair bit.

DAN: I'd call close to a grand a fair bit.

STEVE: Well, that all depends on what you call a fair bit.

DAN: *(Pause.)* So what you doing here then?

STEVE: Eh?

DAN: Why do you come here if you've got a whole gym at home?

STEVE: I got *rid* of it, mate.

DAN: Sold it?

STEVE: Nah, gave it away. Gave it to the kids.

DAN: You've got children?

STEVE: Nah, mate. The kids. The kids in my neighbourhood. It's nice to give something back, you know?

DAN: Right.

STEVE: Yeah, prefer the atmosphere, here, at the Gym. You know, the guys, the banter. At home when you're lifting weights three hours a day it can get a bit monotonous, you know? I mean, I don't do this for the six-pack. I don't do it for the pronounced deltoids, tight pecs and defined quadriceps. No, mate, I do it for the crack.

DAN: The crack. *(STEVE nodding.)* Is that right?

STEVE: You know don't ya? You know what I'm talking about, having a laugh with the lads, having a few beers…having a laugh…a few beers…Yeah, you know, don't ya? You're alright you are. *(Extends hand.)* Steve.

DAN: Dan. *(They shake hands.)*

(Pause.)

STEVE: So, Dan the Man, got a bit of fanny flying round your nozzle?

DAN: I'm sorry?

STEVE: Got a girlfriend, mate?

DAN: No, mate.

STEVE: What, strapping fella like you? Surely there's some bit out there wants to chew on a bone.

DAN: I'm sorry, mate, I really can't understand what you're saying. Do you mean am I sleeping with anybody?

STEVE: Yeah.

DAN: I am actually, yes.

STEVE: She's not your girlfriend, though?

DAN: I'm sorry, have we met?

STEVE: No, mate.

DAN: Right. Didn't think so.

(Pause.)

STEVE: Just a…casual thing is it?

DAN: Yes, I suppose so.

STEVE: Right…What she does she look like?

DAN: Look, mate, I don't want to be rude but I'd quite like to get on with my session so if you don't mind…

STEVE: No, mate you carry on.

(Pause.)

Young, is she?

DAN: Give it a rest, mate.

STEVE: Right you are.

(Workout music.)

STEVE: Behind the redbrick corner, by the bins. I'm watching you. I can see what you're doing. Wading through the fag butt puddles to get a better view, snatching a glance at the both of you, through the pissing grey rain, across the road from Browns. *Browns* for fuck's sake.

TERRY: Hi, I'm Terry. I think I've seen you here before. Do you come here often? You look great.

DAN: Tits, tits, tits, tits…

STEVE: Feeding each other like sexed-up babies. Me by the bins…

TERRY: Hi, I'm Terry.

DAN: … tits, motorbike, tits, tits, tits, rye bread, tits…

TERRY: Hi, I'm Terry. I think I've seen you here before. Do you come here often? You look great.

STEVE: He's touching her. He's fucking touching her underneath the table. Pushing his foot against her sodden knickers, pressing against her. Me with the fag butts…

TERRY: You look great.

DAN: … milk, tits, motorbike, tits,

TERRY: You look great.

DAN: …rye bread, tits, leather, tits…

TERRY: Hi, I'm Terry.

DAN: …tits…

TERRY: You look great.

DAN: …tits…

TERRY: Do you come here often?

STEVE: She's grinding her jaw, grabbing his arm. He grips her back, pins her down to the table, snarls right back at her violent face, she's crushing him close as she comes. Me in the rain by the bins…

DAN: …tits, tits, suck on some cock – what? What the fuck?

TERRY: Hi…

DAN: Tits…

TERRY: …I'm Terry.

STEVE: Bins…

DAN: …tits, girls, yeah, tits, tits, rye bread…

STEVE: He slowly removes his foot from her pants. Tries to look cool as he looks for his sock, and inserts his slippery toes. My feet are wet from the puddles.

TERRY: You look great.

DAN: …tits, have I…have I shat myself? *(Checks.)* Thank fuck for that. Tits, Tits…

STEVE: Sparking up a fag, she looks out the window, straight at me, not seeing me. Me by the bins, and the fag butts.

(They finish together with a grunt/shout. Music cuts.)

STEVE: FAGS!

DAN: TITS!

TERRY: I'M TERRY!

(They rest.)

STEVE: Ooo, think I'm done. Better give the old muscles a rest. Go for a steam, I reckon. Yeah a good old steam. Relax the muscles.Gonna go for a steam. See you in a bit, then, Dan the Man.

(STEVE exits. DAN moves onto the pull-up bar. He does some pull-ups while TERRY watches.)

TERRY: Wow. I can only manage 5.

DAN: Ah? *(Turns to look at TERRY holding on with one arm.)*

TERRY: I can only manage 5.

DAN: Well, you can do what you can do, I suppose.

TERRY: Yeah, I guess. What can you do?

DAN: Sorry?

TERRY: On the bar.

DAN: Depends…Fifteen, twenty. Depends what I've eaten, how much rest I've had.

TERRY: Right.

(DAN resumes pull-ups. Shouting, he doesn't hear TERRY's approaches.)

TERRY: Hi, I'm Terry...You look great.

(DAN hops down from bar. Stretches his arms.)

DAN: Still here, mate?

TERRY: Yeah. Do you mind?

DAN: You've paid your money haven't you?

TERRY: Yeah...

DAN: Well then.

TERRY: Yeah....

(DAN moves over to a different piece of equipment.)

What do you eat?

DAN: What?

TERRY: For the...what do you eat?

DAN: Oh, right. Erm...Fish...vegetables...grilled chicken. Eggs.

TERRY: That's interesting.

DAN: Not really.

TERRY: No it's not is it? It's incredibly boring. Sorry. I'll just... leave you to it.

Cheers...

(TERRY moves away, embarrassed. Starts stretching again.)

DAN: Mate. Mate.

TERRY: Yes?

DAN: Are you alright?

TERRY: I'm fine, thank you.

DAN: OK. You look like you're giving yourself a bit of a hard time over there.

TERRY: I'm not giving myself a hard time, I'm just concentrating – I want to get on.

DAN: You want to get on, do you?

TERRY: Yes.

DAN: Fine, I'll leave you to…get on.

TERRY: Thank you.

(Pause. DAN reflects.)

DAN: Oi. Oi. Get up.

TERRY: I beg your pardon?

DAN: I said get up. I'm going to show you how to do a few pull-ups.

TERRY: I can do pull-ups.

DAN: Yeah. Five.

TERRY: Yes, exactly: five. That's a lot more than most people can manage.

DAN: What? Fat people? I know girls that can do more than that.

TERRY: Lucky them.

DAN: No, not lucky them. They work hard, they eat well, they get results. There's no mystery to it. What are you, mid-thirties?

TERRY: Thirty-one.

DAN: Thirty-one, there you go. You're fit, you're reasonably built –

TERRY: I'm skinny.

DAN: You're lean. You're in good shape, dude.

TERRY: *(Smiling.)* Thank you…

DAN: Jesus…

TERRY: What?

DAN: Nothing, mate. I just mean with your build you should be hitting double figures no problem.

TERRY: I am trying.

DAN: It's not a criticism, mate, it's an observation. Bit touchy are we?

TERRY: Yes I am, particularly when I've got Mr Universe telling me about all the fish and eggs he eats – fascinating as it is – hanging from the bar with one arm like a randy baboon, telling me I should be *"hitting double figures."* Well thank you for your advice, I'll take it on board, but for the moment, I'm perfectly happy –

DAN: Shut up.

TERRY: Excuse me?

DAN: Shut your fucking mouth.

(Pause.)

Get up on the bar.

(Pause.)

Come on then, up you get, let's go.

TERRY: OK. Can I just stretch out a little first –

(DAN stops TERRY from stretching, manhandles him over to the pull-up bar.)

DAN: Bollocks, mate. Up you get.

TERRY: What, now?

DAN: Yes, now.

(DAN "boosts" TERRY onto pull-up bar.)

OK, go on.

(TERRY does one pull-up. Straining.)

DAN: *(Grabs TERRY's midriff.)* OK, first of all, keep this tight.

(During this period of action, STEVE returns, sodden, from the Steam Room offstage. He watches DAN and TERRY momentarily. He then returns to the changing room.)

Legs too, you're swaying all over the place. Good. Now, when you pull up, imagine instead that you're pulling the bar down to meet you. Visualise the ideal you: the you you want to be. Block everything else out. It's just you and the bar. Keep your shoulders down and you'll engage your lats. *(Grabs them.)* Good. This might sound a bit weird but try and suck your arsehole in. It'll keep your trunk tight. And don't forget to breathe. Diaphragm down, shoulders aligned. See, it's easier isn't it?

TERRY: *(Straining.)* Yeah.

DAN: You coming down?

TERRY: *Yeah.*

(DAN supports TERRY back down.)

DAN: Better?

TERRY: Yeah. Much. How d'you know all that stuff?

DAN: Years of practise, mate. It's all about visualisation. *(Points from his eyes to TERRY's.)*

DAN: "Visualisation" *(Repeats motif.)*

TERRY: Visualisation. *(Repeats.)*

DAN: Mr Universe, eh?

TERRY: I'm sorry?

(DAN strikes a body-building pose.)

Oh God, how embarrassing.

DAN: Dan. I'm Dan.

TERRY: Hi Dan.

DAN: What's your name, mate?

TERRY: Dan – Terry.

DAN: Are you sure?

TERRY: *(Laughs.)* I think so. Thanks.

DAN: You already said that, mate.

TERRY: Oh yeah. "Thanks a lot."

DAN: OK. Well…Terry… just give us a shout if you need spotting for anything else. You should be alright on the bar now.

TERRY: Likewise…

DAN: Like what?

TERRY: Likewise…if you need a hand with anything just give me a shout as well.

DAN: OK, mate, I'll let you know.

(DAN goes over to bench press.)

TERRY: What are you doing?

DAN: I'm using the bench press, Terry.

TERRY: Right, yeah, thought so…Do you want a hand?

DAN: What, lifting the bar?

TERRY: No, I mean, would you like me to kiss you?

DAN: No, mate you're alright. Thanks for the offer –

TERRY: I mean, *spot* – spot you. It's dangerous pressing that much without anyone *spotting* you.

DAN: I have used one of these before.

TERRY: I'm sure you have. Look, fine, I'm just saying…if you want someone to…hold it for you…I mean take it from you… then, you know…just give it to me.

DAN: Would you *like* to spot me, Terry?

TERRY: I don't mind, it's up to you.

DAN: That would be great, mate. Come on.

(DAN settles down on the bench press. TERRY "spots" him. Workout music. TERRY drifts off into his own thoughts, throughout which DAN grunts and strains with increasing intensity. Mid-way through, STEVE re-enters and watches.)

TERRY: Don't get a hard-on, don't get a hard-on, don't get a hard-on, don't get a hard-on, don't get a hard-on, don't get a hard-on, don't get a hard-on, no *don't* get a hard-on. Don't get a hard-on, no don't get a hard-on, don't get a hard-on, don't get a hard-on, don't get a hard-on, don't get a hard-on, don't get a hard-on, no *don't* get a hard-on. Don't get a hard-on, don't get a hard-on, don't get a hard-on, don't get a hard-on, don't get a hard-on, don't get a hard-on, don't get a hard-on, no *don't* get a hard-on.

(Music cuts.)

DAN: *(Straining.)* Terry. Terry. Take the fucking bar.

TERRY: What?

DAN: *The bar.*

TERRY: Oh, shit, sorry, Dan.

(Takes the bar; replaces it on the stand. STEVE creeps up behind TERRY and surprises him.)

STEVE: AARGH!

TERRY: AH! *(Recovers himself.)* Jesus fuck, Steve, what the fuck are you playing at!

STEVE: *(Helpless mirth.)*

TERRY: Wanker! Have you got any idea how dangerous that is? I could have dropped the bar on Dan's face, you wouldn't be laughing then would you, you prat? *(To DAN.)* I'm sorry, Dan.

DAN: Don't worry about it.

TERRY: *(To STEVE.)* Dickhead.

STEVE: *(Slowly recovers.)* I'm sorry, I couldn't help it: you looked so serious. Honestly, man, you've got no idea how funny you look from behind.

DAN: Thought you were in the steam room.

STEVE: You thought right. Yes, I was in the steam room, having a *steam*, and then all of a sudden I thought, "Where's Dan?" And then I thought "Where's Terry?" And then it hit me, they're in there together. Alone. Dan has got no idea what danger he's in, I thought. Terry will be in there, "spotting" him at the press bench, one thing will lead to another, and before you know it, Terry will be declaring his manly love for Dan. Maybe the feeling's mutual, I don't know…

(Silence.)

I didn't mean to interrupt anything. If you guys want some more time together just let me know. I'm really happy for you both; I hope it all works out. Just try not to make a mess OK? On the floor. If somebody slips and cracks their head open because of spunk on the floor, I mean,

(To DAN.) the manager wouldn't be very happy about that, now, would he?

(Silence.)

'Cos, you know, in this day and age, that kind of thing's fine. Arse-fucking, I mean. Just don't ask me to join in OK? I like you both as friends I really do, I think you're great. Well, Dan, we've only just met, but you seem like a…really good guy. Quite fit – not in that way. So…yeah. Count me out the threesomes OK, guys?

(Silence.)

Oh come on guys, I'm only joking. You know I love queers, for their dress sense if nothing else. Fuck's sake, lighten up. Only having a laugh. You finished with the press bench, mate?

TERRY: It's called a fucking bench press, Steve.

STEVE: Bench press. *(To DAN.)* You done?

DAN: It's all yours. *(Getting off bench.)*

STEVE: Cheers…You wouldn't mind spotting me would you, mate? *(Gets on to bench.)* It's just I don't quite trust Terry. *(Mock whisper.)* He's a bit of a gay.

DAN: No, mate, I'll spot you.

STEVE: Nice one.

TERRY: Steve, you won't be able to lift it.

STEVE: Pardon me, Terence?

TERRY: It's much heavier –

STEVE: Thank you for the warning, madam, but I think I can handle it. *(Looks up at DAN.)* Ready, big man? *(DAN nods.)* Hand him over, then.

(DAN eases bar down towards STEVE's chest. He collects himself, then pushes, letting out an enormous cry. Lifts the bar halfway. Then falters. DAN grabs the bar.)

DAN: Give it here, mate.

STEVE: *Let fucking go.*

DAN: It's not a competition, mate.

STEVE: *Give me the fucking bar.*

(Process repeats. Even bigger cry.)

TERRY: Steve, it's too heavy.

STEVE: *Fuck off!*

(DAN eases bar back down.)

DAN: I'm taking it off you this time, alright?

(STEVE lifts it three quarters of the way, screaming, then hurts his back. DAN replaces the bar.)

STEVE: …fucking back! *(Sits up.)*

TERRY: Where does it hurt? *(Touches STEVE's back.)*

STEVE: Get off. It's fine. It's fine.

(Gets up and starts doing some squats.)

DAN: Maybe you should give it a rest, Steve. You've got an injury.

STEVE: Yes, I have…in my back. My back isn't in my legs is it? Thanks for the advice, Quincy, but I'd like to get on with some leg-work –

TERRY: Quincy's a pathologist.

STEVE: What?

TERRY: Quincy's a pathologist. He solves crimes by looking at dead people. You're not dead are you?

STEVE: Terry?

TERRY: You're really after someone like, I don't know, James Herriot.

DAN: He's a vet.

STEVE: Yeah, listen to the man, he's a vet.

DAN: I think I'll leave you guys to it.

(DAN moves to another piece of equipment.)

STEVE: *(To TERRY.)* It's not too late, you know. It's never too late in matters of the heart. Go to him, tell him you love him. If you don't say something you'll regret it. Maybe not today, maybe not tomorrow, but one day, soon –

TERRY: Go away.

STEVE: Oh cheer up you miserable prick.

(Workout music.)

STEVE: Twenty feet behind, following the smell of your hot skin as it rises above the Monday morning stench of rush hour. Exhaust fumes and fag buts marinating in puddles. Buses and double yellows and drizzle. Turn another corner and it's fifteen feet now, I can hear the clip clop of your Clarks. The change jangling in your pocket and the leather strap squeak of the Christmas gift brass buckle bag.

DAN: Get up: go for a run. Rehydrate and then prepare breakfast: turkey bacon on rye with poached eggs. Girls with their tits out smiling at me. Allow 45 minutes for digestion then a weightless workout listening to Simply Red. 5 sets of wide arm press ups: 25 reps. Breasts in my mouth and in my hands.

TERRY: I don't want you to say a word. I want to touch you, I want to kiss your chest, nibble every muscle jutting out of your frame.

STEVE: Ten feet from you and I'm out in the open, willing you to turn around and catch me. Turn around and smile, give me the finger, tell me you'll be back around half past six. But you won't turn around; it's like your back won't work. I'm five feet behind you and you're thinking of him, you can smell him in your clothes and your skin.

DAN: Repeat with hands placed together: 18 reps per set. Keep rehydrating in breaks between sets. Lots of breasts bouncing around, casting shadows in the strange light. Hand-stand push ups, bench lifts and pull-ups to follow. Sex with lots of girls who I've never met at the same time all with big breasts that bounce against each other in the strange light.

TERRY: I want to chew on you for breakfast. I want to bring you orange juice and scrambled eggs and while you're doing the crossword I'll wrap my palms around your thick strong cock.

STEVE: I'm matching you now, footstep for footstep, waiting to drag you away.

DAN: Powershake to feed the muscles after the work out, then some steamed fish and vegetables. Rest for thirty minutes then begin abdominal workout. Listen to the Lighthouse Family. Tits in the kichen; on the wall. Three fannies knocking at the door.

TERRY: I'll nuzzle the hair around the base of your penis and slowly, run the tip of my tongue up the seam of your shaft, teeter over the edge and then envelope you into my mouth.

STEVE: I can picture the scene, by some bins, behind a block, with a balaclava hiding my face. I do what I said I would, but you do nothing, just wait for me to finish what I'm doing.

DAN: Swim in the afternoon. Go into the girls changing room and have sex with all the girls. Get home: have a light snack of tabouleh salad. Clean the bike. Have sex with the bike.

TERRY: Suck your fat, rude head till I gag. Suck, suck your bastard straight cock till you come in my desperate mouth.

STEVE: I want you to struggle, to scream, to resist. Instead nothing but taut silence. So I don't do that, I watch you walk on, hoping you'll turn around and see me.

DAN: Dinner: chicken breasts with crème fraiche and some sex with girls. Go to a club on my own, find a girl: have sex.

(Music cuts.)

TERRY: COCK

STEVE: RAPE

DAN: BREASTS

TERRY: What?

DAN: Nothing.

STEVE: No.

TERRY: I don't know.

 (Silence.)

TERRY: Water?

STEVE: Water.

DAN: Water.

 (Silence. They get some water.)

TERRY: Do you come here often?

DAN: I beg your pardon?

STEVE: 'Course he comes here often. Look at him, he's ripped. Look at those pecs, man, like giant steaks on his chest. You don't get def like that sitting on your arse eating chips do you, Dan?

DAN: No, mate.

STEVE: "Do you come here often?" What sort of a question is that? Fuck me, Terry, if I didn't know you better I'd say you were a cock gobbler. I know I forgot, you *are*, aren't you? You like a bit of man pork, don't you? "Do you come here often?" I don't know…

DAN: What's gay about asking me if I come here often?

STEVE: Well, you know, it's gay isn't it?

DAN: No, not really.

STEVE: Well, no but…it's like…you know, the sort of thing you say to a bird in a club. "Do you come here often?"

DAN: Is it? That's not what I say. *(To TERRY.)* Is that what you say?

TERRY: No.

STEVE: Alright Lothario, what do you say?

DAN: "Hi, I'm Dan."

(Pause.)

STEVE: What, you just tell them what your name is?

DAN: Yeah.

STEVE: And that's it?

DAN: Pretty much.

STEVE: Alright, mate, whatever you say.

DAN: OK.

(Pause.)

STEVE: You really just tell them your name?

DAN: Yes.

STEVE: Nothing more?

DAN: She usually tells me her –

STEVE: "Hi, I'm Dan" – yeah, that's really gonna work.

DAN: It seems to.

STEVE: No.

DAN: Yes.

(Pause.)

STEVE: You want to work on your chat-up lines, mate.

DAN: Excuse me?

STEVE: Your chat-up line, your opening gambit, your first attack, your loosener, your USP, your suckerpunch, your fannygrabber, your cuntcatcher, your one-way ticket to the land of quim.

DAN: Sorry, mate, you've lost me.

STEVE: The killer one-liner, to soften 'em up and open them out.

DAN: But that doesn't work.

STEVE: Fucking does mate.

DAN: Women hate that sort of thing.

STEVE: Bollocks, they love it.

DAN: Love what exactly?

STEVE: The gift-of-the-gab, the charm, the panache the self-conf.

(Music and lights suggest club. TERRY and DAN become random women and STEVE alternates between them.)

STEVE: Was your Dad a burglar?

TERRY: You're an arsehole. Fuck off.

(He turns to DAN.)

STEVE: How d'you like your eggs?

DAN: Over easy in bed with my husband. Go away.

(He turns to TERRY.)

STEVE: Do you mind if I ask you a question?

TERRY: If you must…

STEVE: Do you consider yourself to be a strong woman?

TERRY: Yes.

STEVE: Strong enough to resist my mighty sperm?

TERRY: Sorry, I can't hear you

STEVE: Are you strong enough to resist my mighty sperm?

TERRY: *(Pause.)* No, sorry, can you say it again?

STEVE: Are you strong enough to resist my mighty sperm?

(She looks at him, mortified. He turns to DAN and pinches his arse, who turns around.)

Oh my, God, that guy just pinched your arse –

(She slaps him. He turns to TERRY .)

STEVE: Hi, I'm Steve.

TERRY: Hi, Steve. I'm Anna. *(She smiles. She likes him.)*

STEVE: …so…do you come here often?

(Her face drops. Back in the gym.)

DAN: And that works does it?

STEVE: Every time.

TERRY: How often do you go to the clubs, Steve?

STEVE: Oh, you know, sometimes.

TERRY: Steve, you've got a wife.

STEVE: I do.

TERRY: What does she think about you going to the clubs and chatting up the girls?

STEVE: What she doesn't know won't hurt her. Besides, it's hardly a crime to go out and dance with a few girls every now and then, is it?

TERRY: I guess not.

(Pause.)

STEVE: "Do you come here often?" *(Points at TERRY.) Gay!*

DAN: Sorry, do you have a problem with gay people?

STEVE: What?

DAN: Have you got something against gays?

STEVE: Erm…er…

DAN: Do you feel threatened by gay people?

TERRY: Steve?

STEVE: Shut up, Terry.

TERRY: We can take that as a yes can we?

STEVE: Yes – no. Fuck off. What?

DAN: What if I told you I was gay?

TERRY/STEVE: What?

DAN: How would it make you feel if I told you I was gay?

STEVE: But…you…you can't be…not if…you're not are you?

DAN: What?

STEVE: …you know…

DAN: Gay?

STEVE: That's the one.

DAN: No. No I'm not gay. Not any more… I'm joking.

(Pause.)

TERRY: So…*do* you come here often?

DAN: A fair bit, yeah.

TERRY: I bet you do.

STEVE: 'Course he does.

TERRY: Your arms…

STEVE: How else d'you get so stacked?

TERRY: …they're amazing.

STEVE: You've got one hell of a rack dude.

TERRY: Those thighs…

STEVE: You don't get def like that sitting on your arse –

TERRY: …they could crush a man.

STEVE: – eating chips.

TERRY: Your eyes…

STEVE: Look at those pecs…

TERRY: …they're gorgeous

STEVE: …like giant steaks.

TERRY: Those lips…

STEVE: Dan the man…

TERRY: I want to kiss them…

STEVE: The man that can.

TERRY: I want to kiss you.

STEVE: Ladies love Dan.

TERRY: I love you.

STEVE/DAN: What?

TERRY: I love it here, it's so light… Have I seen you here before?

DAN: You might have done, mate.

TERRY: You seem familiar.

STEVE: Do you want to just tug him off now?

DAN: Shut up, Steve, you're embarrassing yourself.

(Pause. DAN resumes working out.)

STEVE: "Hi, I'm Dan". *(Cracks up.)*

DAN: Have you got a point to make?

STEVE: Me? No. No point.

DAN: Then shut it.

STEVE: *OK, Dan.* I'm just fascinated…

DAN: You what?

STEVE: By you. I'm fascinated, by your way with the ladies. I'd love to know how you do it.

DAN: *(To TERRY.)* Is he normally like this?

TERRY: He's had a rough week.

STEVE: It's been hard, Dan, but meeting you has made it all so much better. You're a real swell guy.

DAN: You're starting to piss me off, Steve.

STEVE: *"Hi, I'm Dan."*

(DAN rushes at STEVE. TERRY intercepts him as Cherie and the Club is reprised.)

TERRY: I'm Cherie.

DAN: Hello, Cherie.

TERRY: Hello…Dan.

(Pause. He draws closer.)

DAN: So…?

TERRY: Oh, this is ridiculous.

DAN: What's ridiculous?

TERRY: You can't just come over here and say, "So…?"

DAN: Why not?

TERRY: Because, look just bugger off, OK? You're very rude and I'm very married, so goodbye, it was lovely meeting you, Dan. *(She goes. He grabs her hand and pulls her towards him.)*

DAN: Dance with me.

TERRY: Oh please, it's like a bad film.

DAN: It's good isn't it?

(Back in the gym.)

TERRY: And then what happens?

STEVE: I think we've seen enough, don't you?

TERRY: I want to see the rest

DAN: I take her onto the dance floor.

STEVE: You didn't even buy her a drink?

(Reprise club. They are dancing, DAN behind TERRY, with his hands all over her, kissing her neck.)

TERRY: Stop it.

DAN: What's he called?

TERRY: Who?

DAN: Your husband.

TERRY: Steve.

DAN: Where's Steve tonight?

TERRY: At home; he's got a bad back.

DAN: Poor Steve. I hope he gets better.

TERRY: Stop it, Dan.

DAN: You stop.

(Back in the gym.)

TERRY: And then what happens?

DAN: What do you think?

TERRY: I want you to show me.

(They move in for the kiss, but STEVE interrupts, intervening and taking TERRY with him as he goes, using him as Cherie to graphically illustrate his story.)

STEVE: I think we all know what happens next, don't we? He leads her out of the club, winks at the doorman on his way out. Wolf-whistles a white cab that pulls up without him needing to even check his stride. Opens the door, in she goes and so he follows. In the back seat, orange light flying by: he's whispering into her left ear all the things he's going to do to her in ten minutes time. All fingers and tongues and wetness in the dark. Licking and sucking and fucking till dawn. Then sleep. Deep, calm, satisfied…sleep.

(Pause.)

Then you wake in the morning and you're at it again. Less passionate than before but smug in the dull fuck-ache of screwing until numb.

Avoiding each other's mouths because of the foul morning breath and she smells kind of bad when you're taking her from behind –

TERRY: Alright that's enough –

STEVE: But you carry on pumping her, slowly but surely, with your eye on the clock to see how long you've been going –

TERRY: Steve, can you stop, please?

STEVE: 5 minutes more and you'll have done sixty minutes. Then you can give it to her. Is that what it's like?

DAN: Pretty much.

(Silence. STEVE and DAN staring at one another.)

So you're Steve.

STEVE: Yes I am.

(Silence. TERRY is still squatting in front of STEVE.)

TERRY: Are you two going to have a fight?

DAN: Oh, Terry.

TERRY: Because if you are, I just want you both to know that I'm not going to try and break it up.

STEVE: Shut up, Terry.

TERRY: Well, I'm not. If I get involved I'll get hurt and I don't want to get hurt. I don't want to fight anybody.

STEVE: It's alright, Terry, we're not going to have a fight.

TERRY: Are you sure?

STEVE: Yes.

TERRY: Dan?

DAN: *(Eyes on STEVE.)* What?

TERRY: What about you?

DAN: What about me?

TERRY: Are you going to fight?

DAN: What? *(Turns to TERRY.)* What are you talking about?

TERRY: The fight…

STEVE: Shut up, Terry.

DAN: *(Staring at STEVE.)* What?

STEVE: Me? Nothing. What the fuck do you want?

DAN: What? Fuck off.

STEVE: *(To DAN.)* You fucking snake. You really are quite something aren't you? You bowl in here like a proper Jack the Lad, giving it all the "what would you say if I was gay bollocks", sitting on your fucking bike, going absolutely nowhere, staring at yourself because you can't tear your eyes away from that dick on a stick body of yours, that lumberjack fucking meathead jaw, that throbbing vein bulging in your forehead that you know the girls love because they can see just how hard you *work it*. That beautiful, totem of a body – look at his tits aren't they great? Fuck me, Dan, haven't I seen you on the cover of Men's Health? I mean you just look so damn *good*. That toned, taught physique that gets the girls every time – that gets my wife every time. Speaking of which, how is she, Dan? Does she go like a rocket? I'd love to know. Do send my regards when you see her next. I saw her yesterday actually, where we live, together. She suffers from irritable bowel syndrome, don't you know? It's like having a thousand little men jabbing your belly with spears apparently. The only thing that soothes it is to rub the small of her back. This helps her to fart. I spent three hours last night rubbing her back and stroking her hair while she farted silently in my face. I've got to be honest, Dan, I think it's all that fucking you've been doing. I think you're giving my missus a dicky tummy, and you know, there's only so much back rubbing I can do before…

DAN: Before what, Steve? What exactly are you going to do? Are you going to carry on squealing till someone gives you a cuddle? You little prick, what the fuck are you playing at – are you stalking me? Jesus, I come in here and gay boy over there can't take his sweaty little eyes off of me and you – I've got no idea what's going on with you. Somehow you've tracked me down to this place; you want to be my friend? I'm screwing your wife, mate, it's not going to happen –

STEVE: Hey, I didn't know you were coming here.

DAN: Whatever.

STEVE: If I'd have known you were coming here –

DAN: What? What would you have done? What? Either do something, shut the fuck up, or leave.

TERRY: *Yeah*, Steve.

DAN: Shut up.

TERRY: "*Do something, shut the fuck up, or leave, yeah?*"

DAN: Do you want a slap?

TERRY: Yes I bloody do. Spank me, Daniel!

DAN/STEVE: *(To TERRY.)* Shut up!

STEVE: You shut your fucking mouth, you. You can have your fun with my wife, she'll come back don't you worry, you go ahead. You fucking…fuck her.

DAN: I will. I am. Fuck off.

STEVE: *(Attacks DAN, who grabs him. Ends up hugging DAN, distressed.)*

DAN: Steve…

STEVE: Stay where you are.

DAN: Come on, mate. Maybe you should go home.

STEVE: I'm not going anywhere.

DAN: Come on, get off. *(DAN gently pushes STEVE away.)*

STEVE: Do you love her?

DAN: You what?

STEVE: Do you love her?

DAN: No.

STEVE: Then stop fucking her.

DAN: No.

TERRY: Go home, Steve. Talk to your wife.

STEVE: I don't know what to say. *(Looks at DAN.)*

DAN: What?

(DAN becomes Cherie.)

What is it, Steve, why d'you keep staring at me? *(Moves away.)*

STEVE: How are you?

DAN: …I'm fine, baby…How are you?

STEVE: …Fine…I love you –

(Break out. Back in the gym.)

TERRY: Where's this going, Steve?

STEVE: What?

TERRY: *(Looks at him, bewildered.)*

STEVE: Will you fuck off? I'm trying to talk to my wife.

(Back into embrace.)

STEVE: Can we talk?

DAN: Hm-hm. What about?

STEVE: About us. About you and me.

DAN: OK.

STEVE: I love you, sweetheart.

DAN: I love you too, baby.

STEVE: Good. Good.

DAN: What?

STEVE: Nothing.

DAN: Is that it?

STEVE: Yeah…I guess.

(Pause. They look at each other.)

DAN: What is it, Steve, what do you want me to say?

STEVE: Nothing…I don't want you to say anything, I…

DAN: You keep looking at me like… *(Demonstrates.)* What is that – what does that mean?

STEVE: Nothing, it doesn't mean…I'm allowed to look at you aren't I?

DAN: No.

STEVE: What?

DAN: I'm joking.

STEVE: Oh. Right. Yeah, I just…wanted you to know…how I feel.

DAN: OK. Thank you. That's sweet.

STEVE: You do know don't you?

DAN: Yes.

STEVE: Well, you know, I just…yeah.

(Pause.)

DAN: Can I go now, Steve?

STEVE: Eh?

DAN: I've got to go.

STEVE: Oh. Where you going?

DAN: The gym.

STEVE: Gonna *work out.*

DAN: Yes. That's what I'm going to do.

STEVE: Right. How long you going to be?

DAN: I don't know, honey. A couple of hours, probably.

STEVE: Wow.

DAN: What, Steve?

STEVE: It's a long time, isn't it? Two hours *working out.*

DAN: Not really. I'm going now, babe. *(Kisses him on the forehead.)*

STEVE: Wait. *(Grabs her.)*

DAN: What is it?

STEVE: Come to bed with me.

DAN: I'm just leaving, Steve.

STEVE: Let's go to bed.

DAN: I'm bleeding.

STEVE: Where? Are you OK?

DAN: I'm on my period, Steve.

STEVE: I don't mind.

DAN: Well, *that's* OK, then.

STEVE: I don't.

DAN: I don't want to Steve. I don't feel like it.

STEVE: We can change that. *(Kisses her neck. Grabs her between the legs. She pulls his hand away. STEVE relents.)*

OK. Sorry.

DAN: I'll be back in a bit.

STEVE: I love you.

DAN: Love you too. Bye.

(Back in the gym. They continue looking at each other.)

What? What the fuck are you looking at? Go home.

STEVE: I can't…I can't go home….

TERRY: You can't stay here, man.

STEVE: I can't…Cherie. I'll have to talk to her…I can't…

TERRY: Why not?

STEVE: Because then she'll know that I know, and if she knows that I know… then I'll have to…I don't know what to do.

TERRY: You can't just leave things as they are. Do something. Do anything.

STEVE: Like what?

TERRY: I don't know. Anything.

(DAN gets up and begins to leave.)

STEVE: Where are you going?

DAN: Going home, mate.

STEVE: But…you can't go home now.

DAN: Oh I think I can.

STEVE: But what about…don't you want to do some more training? I've only just started. Terry's only just finished his warm up, haven't you Terry?

DAN: I'm done, mate, I'm going.

STEVE: You only just got here.

DAN: I've lost my enthusiasm. Sorry.

STEVE: But wait – I want to do a few more sets on the press bench.

DAN: Bench press.

STEVE: Bench press – I want to do a few more sets. Will you spot them for me?

DAN: You'll be fine on your own.

STEVE: No I won't. I need you.

DAN: Terry'll do it won't you, Terry? He likes spotting people.

TERRY: Fuck off, Dan *(Doing pull-ups.)*

DAN: Maybe he won't.

STEVE: Fuck Terry, he'll drop the bloody bar on my face. You know what he's like, old chick pea fingers over there. I'll be going home in an ambulance if you leave me with him. *(To TERRY.)* Only joking mate.

Actually while we're all here why don't you show us some *stretching?*

Go on, give us a whirl. *(To DAN.)* You haven't seen this, have you, mate? It's an absolute classic. *(Mimics.)* "Breathe in…and out…and in –

DAN: I'll see you then, Terry. *(TERRY ignores him.)*

STEVE: *(To DAN.)* Come on, Dan the Man, we're a team, you and me.

DAN: How are we a *team?*

STEVE: Well, you know…we've got the same taste in women… It's a joke.

DAN: Yeah. I'm done, Steve. I'm out of here.

STEVE: Where are you going?

DAN: Not this again.

STEVE: Where?

DAN: Where d'you think?

STEVE: Are you seeing Cherie?

TERRY: *(Drops down from bar.)* Of course he's fucking seeing Cherie.

STEVE: I wasn't asking you.

TERRY: Oh would you prefer "Dan the Man" to tell you?

STEVE: Go fuck yourself you little faggot. Come on, Dan, stay. Let's train for a bit.

DAN: I'm going.

STEVE: No.

DAN: Yes.

STEVE: Please. *Please.*

(*DAN grabs STEVE by the throat.*)

DAN: Stop squealing like a fucking pig.

STEVE: I'm sorry.

DAN: Shut up.

STEVE: *I'm sorry!*

DAN: Shut the fuck up you runt. Come on, Steve hit me. That's what you've been wanting to do since the second I walked in this place, isn't it? You've had it all planned out. You don't say a word. You walk straight up to me and then bam *(Mimes head butt at STEVE.)* right on the nose bridge. Feel that slender bit of cartilage splinter under your forehead and my warm blood shower down your face. Now I'm ready, now I'm scared. My eyes are trying to make friends with me, pleading like a puppy, confused and upset. I don't want any trouble, I didn't know anything about you – bam, bam, bam, shut the fuck up you runt. I'm on my knees now, I'm crying. You stick your chin in my face and say, "Hit me. Fucking hit me," but I'm too much of a pussy to even do that. You're going to kick me in the face. You're going to smash your foot into my big horrible face. Bam. The blood splatters thick against the bench press as I flip backwards. Out cold now, and you're standing over me screaming, "CUNT, CUNT, CUNT!" So come on, Steve. Fucking do it you miserable cunt.

STEVE: No, I don't want to.

DAN: Just there. Go on. *(Sticks his face in STEVE's, eyes closed, pointing to his chin. TERRY is squealing like a pig. To TERRY.)* What the fuck are you laughing at?

TERRY: *(Raises his fists and makes mock battle cry.)* RAAAARGHHHH!

STEVE: …I can't.

DAN: Why not?

STEVE: I don't want to make you angry.

DAN: I'm not angry, Steve, I'm bored.

TERRY: *"I'm not angry, Steve, I'm bored."*

DAN: *(To TERRY.)* What the fuck is your problem?

TERRY: RAAAARGHHHH!

DAN: Are you taking the piss?

TERRY: RAAAARGHHHH!

DAN: You taking the piss out of me?

TERRY: *(Squeals like a pig.)*

DAN: Right come here, I'm going to kick your arse, you little prick.

(DAN, chases TERRY around the gym. TERRY is hysterical, roaring at DAN intermittently, who incensed, continues to pursue him. STEVE shouts at them. They're all shouting at each other.)

TERRY: RAAAARGHHHH!

DAN: You think that's funny do you?

TERRY: RAAAARGHHHH!

DAN: You'll see how fucking funny you are. Come here you little bastard.

STEVE: What the fuck are you doing? Stop chasing each other, this is ridiculous.

TERRY: Run away, Steve! He's going to beat us up. He's going to kill us!

STEVE: Shut up, Terry!

DAN: Stop fucking running away!

STEVE: Stop chasing him!

DAN: Shut up!

STEVE: You shut up!

TERRY: Everybody shut up!

DAN/STEVE: Shut up!

TERRY: RAAAARGHHHH!

STEVE: Jesus, Terry.

TERRY: I can't help it. He won't stop chasing me!

STEVE: Then stop fucking running!

TERRY: Good advice, Steve!

DAN: Come here you little fuck!

TERRY: No, I'm fine where I am, thank you, Dan.

STEVE: Stop! Just fucking stop it for Christ's sake!

TERRY/DAN: Shut up!

STEVE: What do you mean, "Shut up?"

TERRY/DAN: Shut up!

STEVE: Go fuck yourselves.

TERRY: RAAAARGHHHH! Let's fuck ourselves! Come on, guys that's what we came here to do: to fuck! Let's do some fucking! Come on, Dan. Come over here and stick your big fat cock up my arse!

DAN: Shut him up!

STEVE: *You* shut him up!

DAN: He's *your* friend!

STEVE: So?

TERRY: RAAAARGHHHH!

DAN: Do something!

STEVE: Shut your eyes.

DAN: What?

STEVE: *(Grabs DAN.)* SHUT YOUR FUCKING EYES!

(They all stop. DAN adopts Cherie's persona, eyes shut, holding STEVE's hand.)

STEVE: Shut your eyes.

DAN: What's going on, Steve?

STEVE: Just keep your eyes shut.

DAN: I'm cold.

STEVE: Just hang on. I'm being romantic. Now then. I want you to cast your mind back to when we first met. Do you remember?

DAN: Sheena's twenty-first.

STEVE: Sheena's twenty-first – well no we actually met once before that but…Sheena's twenty-first. What did you think when you first saw me?

DAN: I quite fancied your mate actually.

STEVE: Terry?

DAN: Oh he was lovely. Utterly gay, though. Pity.

STEVE: Yeah…anyway…

DAN: Steve, I'm cold, can we go inside?

STEVE: In a minute. I'm nearly done.

DAN: This better be good.

STEVE: Oh it's very good, don't worry. Anyway, when I first clapped eyes on you, it was like the room made a jump cut. Everything was amplified, the colours more intense, the music louder – I'd fallen in love with you. I knew right then that nothing would ever be the same and that I would have to make you mine. And I did. Cherie, my breath, my soul, my everything, will you marry me –

(TERRY breaks the scenario. Back in the gym.)

TERRY: Just fucking hit him, Steve.

STEVE: I don't want to OK, is that such a bad thing? I don't want to. I know that I'm supposed to smash you in the face with that dumb bell, and shout something mean while I kick your fucking head in. I know I'm supposed to go back and get the girl, tell her it's alright: I sorted that dufus out, that I forgive her and lets live happily ever after and grow old and fat together but it's not going to happen, OK?

IT'S NOT GOING TO HAPPEN!

TERRY: What is going to happen, Steve?

STEVE: Nothing needs to happen – why does anything need to happen?

TERRY: Because he's been sleeping with your wife…

STEVE: Yes.

TERRY: …and you're really angry about it…

STEVE: No.

TERRY: …he's *still* sleeping with your wife…

STEVE: Not necessarily.

TERRY: …and you don't want to do anything.

STEVE: …and your point is?

TERRY: That's really weird, Steve.

STEVE: If you're that bothered why don't *you* do something?

TERRY: He's not sleeping with my wife.

STEVE: You haven't got a wife.

TERRY: But you have. *(To DAN.)* And he's having sex with her.

STEVE: Thanks, mate.

TERRY: It's alright, mate.

DAN: I don't believe you. I don't believe you, Steve. I think you *do* want to smash that dumb bell into my face, then stamp on my jaw until it breaks. I think you want to spit in my face, kick me in the back of the head, then go home fuck the life out of your wife. Go on, Steve, do it. Hit me. Fucking hit me.

TERRY: *"Fucking hit me."*

STEVE: Shut up, Terry!

DAN: I won't come back at you, I promise.

STEVE: You will.

DAN: I won't.

STEVE: You will, I know you will. You say that now but you'll change your mind. You'll get angry and you'll smash my face in and then you'll hurt Terry when he tries to stop you –

TERRY: I said I wouldn't get in the way –

STEVE: Shut up – then I'll have to tell Cherie and she mustn't know. She absolutely mustn't know that I know and she definitely can't know that you know that I know. It's the only thing that matters –

DAN: Fuck Cherie.

STEVE: Fuck Cherie?

DAN: Fuck her. She's not here. This is about you and me, Steve. Do it. Hit me.

STEVE: This is like a bad film.

DAN: It's good isn't it?

STEVE: Stop it, Dan.

DAN: You stop…Come on.

(STEVE shapes up to hit him and crumbles, resting his head on DAN's chest. TERRY moves under the pull-up bar starts doing some pull-ups. DAN gently pushes STEVE away who sits, dissolute.)

What the bloody hell is that? You're all over the place. Come on, man, keep this tight here. *(Grabs TERRY's midriff.)* You like that don't you?

TERRY: Take your fucking hands off me, Dan.

DAN: Don't play hard to get, Terry. *(Fondles TERRY's bottom.)* Come on, you love it, don't you? You love it you little tart. *Oh yes.*

TERRY: If you don't stop doing that I'm going to rip your throat out with my teeth.

DAN: *Oh yes –*

(TERRY hops down from the bar and kisses DAN. Then pushes him away.)

TERRY: Fucking queer.

DAN: Why d'you…what?

TERRY: What, did you like it…? *(Laughs.)* So fucking curious. *(Fondles DAN's groin.)* You want to fuck everybody don't you, Daniel? Stick your dick in any hole you can find. You want to fuck Cherie don't you? With your big firm cock. You want to fuck me don't you, Daniel? You'd love to know how all that works. What goes where? Who comes first? To have your cock sucked by another guy. By me. To suck some cock yourself. Swallow another guy's come.

Wouldn't that be fun, wouldn't that be interesting? It's just killing you, the curiosity isn't it? You've never quite managed to kick that naughty little thought out of your mind, what *would* it be like? All those women you've had squirming underneath you, all those tits, all that hair. But in the back of your mind it's always been there hasn't it? What else is there that I could fuck? You'd fuck yourself if you could, wouldn't you Dan? Now there's a thought. So how about it Dan the Man? How about we just go for it over the bench here?

DAN: Yeah…OK

TERRY: *(Laughs.)* "*Yeah. OK*"

DAN: But…

TERRY: That's why I've been coming here, to get a good look at you. I've been thinking about all things I wanted to do to you. Here. In this room. You've kept me awake at night, Dan. You've made me touch myself. I've come thinking about sucking you off while you lift weights. These weights here. *(Bench press.)* Isn't that sad? I can't help it, Dan. I can't get you out of my mind. *(Stops fondling.)* I'm sure you can finish yourself off.

DAN: But…

TERRY: Fuck off.

(DAN exits into changing area and masturbates.)

STEVE: What the fuck are you doing?

TERRY: Sorry?

STEVE: What was that?

TERRY: I thought I was doing you a favour.

STEVE: What the fuck was that, Terry?

TERRY: What's the matter, Steve, are you jealous?

STEVE: You're sick, man.

TERRY: Sick? It's the most fun I've had in weeks.

STEVE: Is he? What is he?

(DAN climaxes next door.).

STEVE: Is he?

TERRY: I don't know Steve. Maybe he *is* a little bit. Shall we ask him?

STEVE: Go fuck yourself.

TERRY: Isn't it past your bed time, Stephen?

STEVE: *(Squares up to TERRY.)* What? What the fuck d'you say to me?

TERRY: Steve –

STEVE: Always got something to say haven't you, you little faggot?

(TERRY laughs.) Always got some bitchy little comment up your sleeve to pull out when you're feeling *particularly* insulted. And you think just because everybody knows you're a dirty little poof, they're not going to smash your smarmy fucking face in –

TERRY: Fuck off, Steve –

STEVE: You want to call me a cunt? You want to call Steve fuck-it-up Watson a cunt? Then here's your chance. The rest of the world's having a pop right now; I'd hate for you to miss out.

TERRY: I'm always calling you a cunt.

STEVE: *(Grabs TERRY by the throat.)* Then say it now. Say "Steve, you're a cunt."

TERRY: Steve, you're hurting me.

STEVE: Do it.

TERRY: Get off. This is ridiculous. What, are you going to beat me up?

STEVE: Cunt.

TERRY: Gonna smack me one, Steve?

STEVE: Say it.

TERRY: Teach this little faggot a lesson?

STEVE: Say it.

TERRY: Fucking cunt.

(*STEVE punches TERRY. They are both appalled.*)

TERRY: Why d'you do that? Why d'you do that Steve? YOU BASTARD!

WHY D'YOU FUCKING HIT ME?

(*Pause.*)

STEVE: (*Distressed.*) I'm sorry, Terry. I didn't mean…I'm sorry, I'm so sorry…

(*TERRY comforts him. As they break the embrace STEVE tries to kiss TERRY, who turns his head.*)

TERRY: No. No.

(*Silence. They both sit on different pieces of equipment. DAN re-enters.*)

DAN: She's not in love with me.

STEVE: You what?

DAN: Cherie. She doesn't love me. It's just sex. We just have sex.

STEVE: Great.

TERRY: Still here, Dan?

DAN: Yeah, I thought maybe we could go for a beer or something.

TERRY: Hm. Sounds like fun. Steve? *(Non-committal response.)*

DAN: Anyway…I'm going…so if anyone wants to…OK.

STEVE: What about my wife?

DAN: Maybe you should talk to her.

STEVE: Yeah.

DAN: OK…See you then.

(DAN exits. Silence as TERRY packs up. DAN re-enters.)

DAN: What team do you support?

STEVE: Team?

DAN: Football. What team do you support?

STEVE: What are you talking about?

DAN: Football.

STEVE: What about it?

DAN: Which team do you support?

STEVE: …Crystal Palace.

(Pause.)

DAN: Brentford…I support Brentford…somebody's got to…. *(To TERRY.)* Do you like football?

TERRY: Sorry, are you talking to me?

DAN: Yeah.

TERRY: What?

DAN: Sorry?

TERRY: What is it?

DAN: What's what?

TERRY: What are you trying to say to me?

DAN: Do you like football?

TERRY: Not really, no.

DAN: Basketball?

TERRY: *What?*

DAN: Do you like basketball?

TERRY: Erm…I do quite like it, yes.

DAN: Same…you're quite tall – above average. Do you play?

TERRY: Do I *play?*

DAN: Basketball. Do you play?

TERRY: No.

DAN: *(To STEVE.)* What about you? Steve. Do you play basketball?

STEVE: No.

DAN: Snooker?

TERRY: *(Quietly.)* Why don't you fuck off, Dan?

DAN: OK. See you.

(DAN exits.)

TERRY: Do you want a lift?

STEVE: What am I going to say to her?

TERRY: Still thinking about that, are you?

STEVE: What am I going to say?

TERRY: Why don't you tell her what happened today? That'd be a start. Be gentle with her, Steve, eh?

(TERRY exits.)

STEVE: I know…about Dan. I met him…at the gym. I've been following you…and him…the restaurant…I was by the bins…the fag butts…I went to the gym…he was there…I wanted me to hit him…I hit Terry…Terry kissed him…I tried to kiss Terry…anyway…I love you…and I want to make everything better… I'm going to get back in shape…Going to be sexier…have more sex with you… if you want…it's up to you really….Do you love him…? I don't think he loves you…I asked him…I don't think he does….is it just the sex…? Because I can do that…I can get better…at the sex…if you want…it's up to you really…. Is that what all this is about…? Or is it about something else…? Anyway…I love you…so what d'you reckon?

(STEVE goes to the bench press and lowers the bar down onto his chest. Begins to lift. Lights fade as he struggles.)

END